WONDER BOOK!

A JOURNAL FOR YOUR CURIOSITIES

ART + BOOKS + NATURE

WELCOME TO YOUR WONDERBOOK:

an interest-led learning tool for you and your child to record and investigate the wonder-full questions they ask.

Learning happens most efficiently when we are interested in the subject, and luckily kids are naturally fascinated and curious about the world around them. The Wonderbook provides a space to honor their interests & maximize deep learning.

By getting deliberate in pursuing their natural curiosities we can support their sense of wonder & capitalize on the benefits of interest-led learning. When the Wonderbook is filled, it serves as a delightful compilation & celebration of all the fabulous questions and curiosities you and your child(ren) have explored together.

HOW TO USE YOUR WONDERBOOK:

If we listen for it, we'll notice that our kids are asking pretty great questions all the time. Most of the time the awe-some "I wonder" pops up when we are in the middle of something else, and often we cannot immediately give their questions the thoughtful response they deserve. The first pages of your Wonderbook offer space to write down these wonder filled questions, so they can be investigated and explored together later. You may wish to use this space as a table of contents as well, by writing the corresponding page number where the topic is explored in the Wonderbook.

The remaining pages of the Wonderbook offer space for your child to draw, along with space to make notes about your discoveries. The grid paper page can be used for additional notes, print-outs, graphs, or pictures.

Some considerations for successful & delightful **WONDERBOOKING**:

- Allow the child(ren) to choose the topic, and set out to explore it with a sense of wonder, and allow yourselves to be surprised!
- Invite the child(ren) to write entries, but consider acting as the scribe if the child is not interested in writing. This allows the child to focus on the exciting content that you're exploring, as well as the process of learning, rather than the mechanics of handwriting and spelling.
- A helpful prompt: consider using a 'question sandwich' to begin and end each topic.

   > Start with: "What do you already know or assume about the topic?"
   > And then, after exploring and researching:
   > "How did your previously held assumptions check out against our research?"

- Utilize a multimedia approach:
  - Print out pictures or maps of what you've discovered to paste in.
  - Invite the child to paint pictures to paste into the illustration space.
  - Take photographs of the child(ren) exploring the topic and add them to the book (this can help kids recall their explorations fondly; which reinforces learning and inspires further exploration).
- A final tip: find something that excites YOU about the topic. Child(ren) are quite good at imitating their grown-ups; you can capitalize on this by getting into the wonder with them! Paint, draw, or write an entry in your own Wonderbook as a gentle invitation for them to get interested in the process.

Here's to enjoying and exploring our world together, with child-like wonder!

HAPPY WONDERBOOKING TO YOU AND YOURS,

   –Johanna Preis, MS, LMFT
   Creator of the Wonderbook, in collaboration with schoolnest

Find Johanna on instagram: @its.a.wonder.led.life
Email: wonder.led.life@gmail.com
Join the fun: use #wonderbooking to share and see other families Wonderbooking.

I WONDER...

PAGE # I WONDER...

I WONDER...

PAGE #

I WONDER...

I WONDER...

I WONDER...

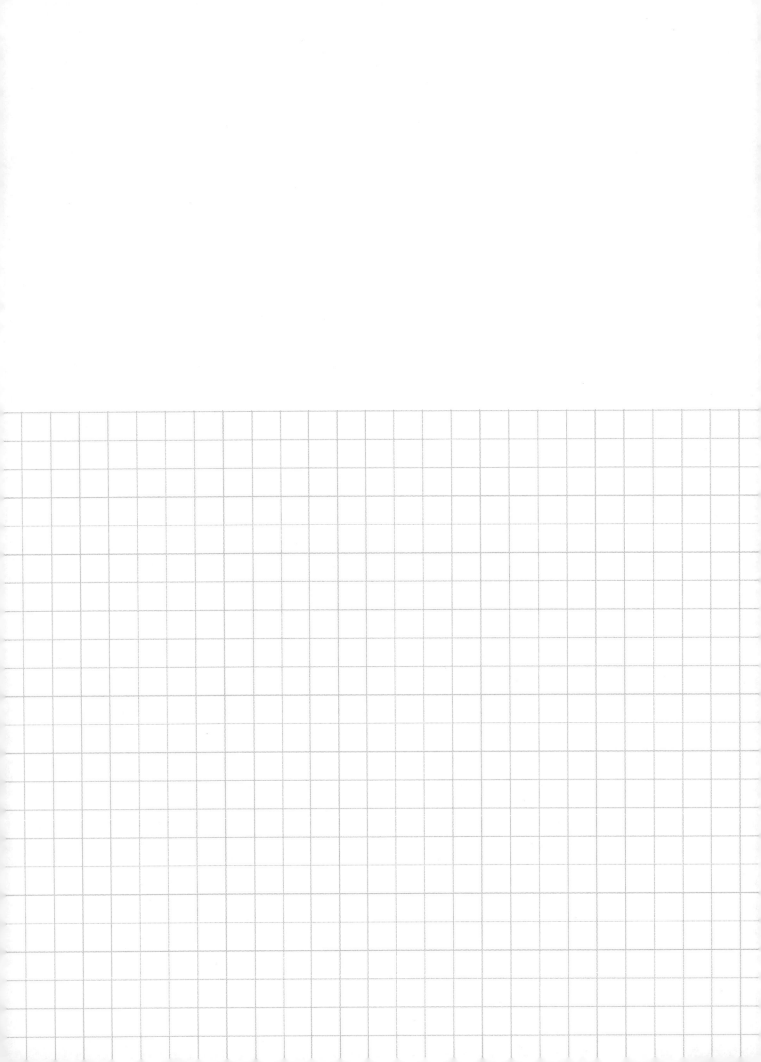

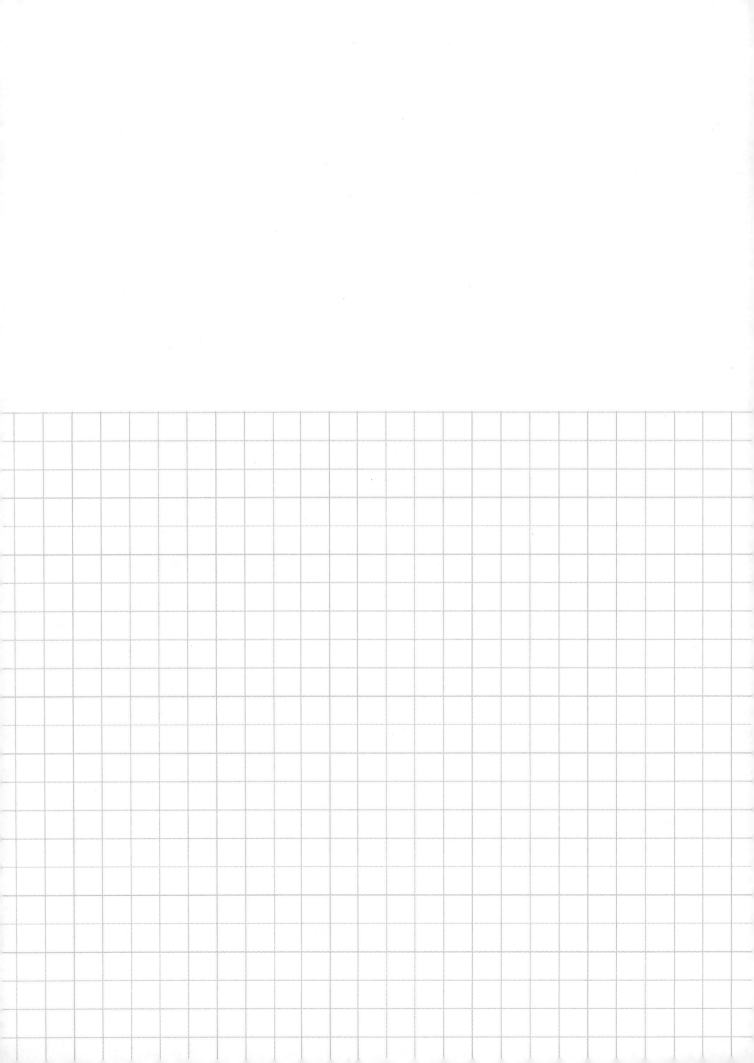

Thank you for purchasing
a schoolnest notebook!

You can find a rainbow of notebook options
in many school subjects (math, spelling,
history timeline, science, grade level
composition books, journals, and more) on:

theschoolnest.com!

Follow along on Instagram @schoolnest

Made in the USA
Middletown, DE
28 August 2022

72511989R00113